Some pesky crooks have taken a load of jewels! After them!

Police
in Action

Welcome, LEGO fans!

LEGO® minifigures show you the world in a unique nonfiction program.

This book is part of a program of LEGO® nonfiction books, with something for all the family, at every age and stage. LEGO nonfiction books have amazing facts, beautiful real-world photos, and minifigures everywhere, leading the fun and discovery.

To find out more about the books in the program, visit www.scholastic.com.

ISBN 978-1-338-28342-6

10 9 8 7 6 5 4 3 2 1   18 19 20 21 22

Printed in the U.S.A.   40
First edition, September 2018

POLICE

Computers on board can record speed and check car license plates.

Emergency! There's been a robbery! The police car is on its way!

POLICE

Police cars have fast engines, extra-bright headlights, and super-tough tires. Flashing blue lights and a siren tell people the police are on the way.

Some of the crooks are up ahead. There's the truck!

Got you! Where are the jewels? This van is full of pizzas!

Yum! At least I got a slice of the action!

Build it!

Build a super-speedy police motorcycle to weave in and out of traffic.

Traffic ahead! A police motorcycle can weave through a traffic jam more easily than a police car.

A switch on my handlebars turns on the lights and siren during a high-speed chase.

POLICE

06

POLICE

Some police motorcyles can reach speeds of 100 miles per hour (160 km/h) in 10.55 seconds. Officers use radios in their helmets to talk to each other.

That crook has some stolen jewels. He's on foot. Hop on the motorcycle!

Oh no! It looks like he's going to steal a vehicle . . .

He's taken a bicycle. Ha! Too slow this time! You're under arrest!

The police need
an eye in the sky. A
helicopter can hover
over the action. It can
guide police units on the
ground, or on water, to their targets.

Some police helicopters have cameras that can see where people are, even at night. The cameras also take photos or videos.

Build it!
Build a police helicopter and police cars and create your own police chase.

Powerful searchlights on the helicopter can follow crooks at night.

Arggh! These pesky police are everywhere!

Police officers must choose the right transportation for the job they have to do.

In large crowds, a police horse may be the best way to move around. Police horses are trained to be very calm, and officers riding them have an awesome view.

Build it!
Build a stable for your police horses, or maybe camels, to live in.

Need to sniff out crooks? Bring in police dogs.

Many police dogs have received medals for their brave work.

German Shepherd dogs are often used by the police. Their sense of smell is 50 times more powerful than a human's. They are used for sniffing out people and objects.

Build it!

Build a police boat for your divers so they can dive for stolen jewels!

The dogs have followed their noses to the river. It's time for the police divers to get into their scuba gear.

It's a tough job. Police divers often search through the night in the cold and dark. They may have to swim through weeds or garbage.

OK, divers, you won't be able to see much, you'll have to feel around.

I've found something! It's a safe! It must be the stolen jewels!

I've found something too! Oh! It's just a rusty old bicycle . . .

Police boats patrol along rivers and coasts, watching for crooks or pirates.

After him! He's wanted for robbery.

He's also driving that Jet Ski way too fast!

Ha! You'll never catch me!

POLICE

T287

These small boats have powerful engines for high-speed chases. They may also rescue people and help fight fires on the water.

Build it!
Build a police boat, ready for action!

Build it!

Build a police Jet Ski. How fast can it go?

Quick and easy to move, Jet Skis can be used by police on the coast and on large lakes and rivers.

A Jet Ski can reach speeds of 70 miles per hour (110 km/h). It can zoom in and out of narrow channels and shallow water. Up to three people can ride at a time!

Just a bit farther and I'm free!

Aaargh! Are these sharks working for the police, too?

Good catch! Great work, sharks!

The police have caught a bunch of crooks. Great work! They need a truck to move them to the police station or prison.

A police van may have small rooms inside, like little cells. Crooks may be handcuffed for their journeys. There's no escaping now!

It's quiet on the road.

Use your stickers to turn the scene into a police chase!

If you can't do the time—don't do the crime!

Glossary

crime
An action that breaks the law and is punished.

crook
A person who breaks the law or who is dishonest.

handcuffs
Metal bracelets that lock around the wrists, used by police to stop crooks escaping.

Jet Ski
A fast water scooter.

license plate
A small metal sign with a unique combination of letters and numbers on it, fixed to the front and back of a road vehicle. It is used to identify the vehicle.

officer
A person in the police force.

patrol
Keeping watch over an area by often traveling around it.

police unit
A small group of police officers working together.

robbery
Stealing money or objects from someone or some place.

searchlight
A super-powerful, extra-bright beam of light that can be turned in any direction. Police use it outside to help find people or objects in the dark.

siren
A super-loud warning bell.

stables
The building where horses are kept and looked after.

transportation
How people or things move about. For example, by bus, train or on horseback.

Credits

The publishers would like to thank:
For the LEGO Group: Randi Kirsten Sørensen, Senior Editorial Coordinator; Paul Hansford, Creative Publishing Manager; Martin Leighton Lindhardt, Publishing Graphic Designer; and Heidi K. Jensen, Business Manager.
For their help in making this book:
Neal Cobourne, John Goldsmid, Shari Joffe, Rachel Phillipson, Ali Scrivens, and Bryn Walls.
Photos ©: cover police car: ALAMTX/Alamy Images; cover background: Splash News/Alamy Images; 1: zodebala/iStockphoto; 2-3 background: onlyyouqj/iStockphoto; 2-3 police car: marcyano/Shutterstock; 3 top: southerlycourse/iStockphoto; 4: zodebala/iStockphoto; 5 top right: alex-mit/iStockphoto; 6-7 background: Martin Brayley/Alamy Images; 6: onlyyouqj/iStockphoto; 7 top right: Andrei Berezovskii/iStockphoto; 8-9 bottom background: VanderWolf Images/Shutterstock; 8-9 top background: onlyyouqj/iStockphoto; 8-9 top helicopter: southerlycourse/iStockphoto; 10: Ben Oliver/Alamy Images; 12 center: John Roman Images/Shutterstock; 12-13 background: Jonathan Salmi/EyeEm/Getty Images; 14-15 background: Tylinek/iStockphoto; 15 top right: Berenika_L/iStockphoto; 16-17: cmart7327/iStockphoto; 18: Polifoto/iStockphoto; 20 bottom: Adrian Reynolds/Shutterstock; 20 top background: hadynyah/iStockphoto; 21 top right: Rupert Weidemann/iStockphoto; 22-23 background: zyxeos30/iStockphoto; 22 bottom: BrianAJackson/iStockphoto.

All LEGO illustrations and stickers by Paul Lee.